The Newborn King

From the Book of Luke
Adapted by Cindy Robertson
Illustrated by Pat Thompson

THE NEWBORN KING
Copyright © 2002 Dalmatian Press, LLC

Published in 2010 by Piggy Toes Press,
an imprint of Dalmatian Publishing Group
Atlanta, GA 30329
No part of this book may be reproduced or copied in any form
without the written permission of Piggy Toes Press.

ISBN: 1-61524-366-6
Printed in Guangzhou, Guangdong, China

10 11 12 GFC 35780 10 9 8 7 6 5 4 3 2

*T*his is the story of the birth of Jesus as told in the second chapter of Luke in the New Testament.

In ancient times, the Roman ruler ordered a count to be taken of all the people who lived in the Roman Empire. Each person went to the town where they were born to be counted.

A man named Joseph left his home in Nazareth and traveled to Bethlehem. His wife, Mary, who was expecting her first baby, went with him.

While they were in Bethlehem, Mary gave birth to a baby boy. They were staying in a stable because there were no rooms left for them to rent. Mary wrapped the baby in a soft blanket and placed him on the straw in the manger.

Outside of the city, shepherds were sleeping in the fields so they could protect their flocks of sheep. God sent an angel to tell the shepherds the great news, but the angel was shining so brightly that the shepherds were afraid.

The angel spoke to the shepherds and told them he was bringing them wonderful news that was for all the people on earth.

"Today in the town of David, a Savior has been born to you; he is Christ the Lord. This will be a sign to you: You will find a baby wrapped in cloth and lying in a manger."

Suddenly more angels appeared and they were all praising God and saying, "Glory to God in heaven, and on earth peace to all men who believe in Him."

After the angels returned to heaven, the shepherds hurried to Bethlehem to see this newborn baby.

There they found Joseph, Mary, and the baby, who was lying in the manger just like the angel had told them.

The shepherds were so amazed by all this that they told everyone they saw about the wonderful new baby.

Mary was happy. She kept these memories and treasured them in her heart.

Returning to the fields, the shepherds were happy and praising God for all the wonderful things they had heard and seen.

This special event is the reason we celebrate Christmas.